WINTER WARMERS

60 COSY COCKTAILS FOR AUTUMN AND WINTER

JASSY DAVIS

ILLUSTRATED BY SARAH FERONE

HarperCollins*Publishers*

Dedicated to distant friends.

And for Jodi Morrison, who taught me how to order a martini.

HarperCollins*Publishers*
1 London Bridge Street
London SE1 9GF
www.harpercollins.co.uk

First published by HarperCollins*Publishers* in 2020

1 3 5 7 9 10 8 6 4 2

Copyright © 2020 HarperCollins*Publishers*
Written by Jassy Davis
Cover and interior illustrations by Sarah Ferone
Cover and interior design by Jacqui Caulton

Jassy Davis asserts the moral right to be
identified as the author of this work

A catalogue record for this book is
available from the British Library

ISBN 978-0-00-840200-6

Printed and bound in Latvia

DISCLAIMER: The publisher urges readers to drink responsibly.

This book features recipes that include the optional use
of raw eggs. Consuming raw eggs may increase the risk of
food-borne illness. Individuals who are immunocompromised,
pregnant or elderly should use caution. Ensure eggs are
fresh and meet local food-standard requirements.

MIX
Paper from
responsible sources
FSC™ C007454

FSC
www.fsc.org

This book is produced from independently certified FSC™ paper
to ensure responsible forest management.

For more information visit: www.harpercollins.co.uk/green

Contents

Introduction

Cocktails don't have a season. They are a year-round delight. And yet, there is something about the shift from warmer to colder weather that makes cocktails more appealing. Perhaps it's because we go out less, preferring to stay tucked up at home while the temperature drops, the rain falls and the nights grow dark. Cuddled up on the sofa or sprawled in front of a fire, a cocktail somehow feels right.

This book is devoted to those cocktails that make the colder months of the year more welcoming. There are hot drinks, including classic mulled wines, spiked hot chocolates and boozy coffees. There are also ice-cold Martinis, indulgent dessert drinks and more than a few riffs on the Negroni. For holiday parties there are punches, eggnogs and spritzes. And there are a few drinks that can only be described as very silly indeed. In the gloomiest depths of winter, when the wind bites and there seems no hope of ever seeing the sun again, mixing an over-the-top nonsense drink is cheering and delightful. I make no apologies for having fun.

If you're new to cocktail making, you'll find guides on how to set up a home bar and basic cocktail-making techniques. If you've already mastered the Manhattan and can make a Sidecar blindfolded, then there are plenty of new drinks and recipes gathered from around the world to offer you some fresh inspiration. Whatever has brought you to this book, please now pull on your cosiest sweater, put some glasses in the freezer to chill and enjoy the best drinks that autumn (aka fall) and winter can provide.

The Right Tools for the Job

You don't need a lot of specialist equipment to make cocktails at home. You can shake drinks in jam jars, stir them in water jugs and measure with teaspoons, bottle caps and that most old-fashioned of things, your eye. But if you want to get a little serious, then there are a few bar tools you can buy to help you become a cocktail king or queen.

MIXING GLASS

When you're stirring cocktails, like Manhattans and Martinis, you want a mixing glass that is wide enough to let you keep the bar spoon moving and deep enough to contain the cocktail without it spilling over the top. A mixing glass with a heavy base is more stable and won't topple over if you get a bit vigorous. Etched mixing glasses provide a bit more grip, so the glass is less likely to slip out of your hand when you pour out the drinks. A spout will also make life easier.

BAR SPOON

To go with your mixing glass, you'll need a bar spoon. These are long-stemmed spoons that typically have a 2.5–5ml (½–1 teaspoon) bowl and a twisted stem. There are three types of bar spoon: American, European and Japanese. American bar spoons are the simplest, with a rubber cap on the end of the spoon and a twisted section in the middle. They are good, basic spoons if you're starting out and just want something to stir drinks with. European bar spoons often have round flat discs at the end, which can be used to muddle soft fruits. The stems are twisted all the way down, and you can use them to layer drinks by trickling the spirit down the stem. Japanese bar spoons tend to have teardrop- or pearl-shaped tips and are much longer than their American and European counterparts, making them a lot more theatrical and elegant to use. One for the showmen among you.

JIGGER

A jigger is an hourglass-shaped measurer that has two measuring bowls – the standard jigger (45ml/1½fl oz) and the pony (30ml/1fl oz). These are the basic measurements for cocktail making. For more specific measuring, you can buy small measuring glasses that are marked up with millimetres, fluid ounces, tablespoons and teaspoons.

SHAKER

There are three types of shaker on the market:
- The cobbler shaker is the three-part metal shaker you are most likely to see in your local homewares store. It breaks down into a shaking tin, a fitted lid with a strainer built in and a cap. Because of the integral strainer, the cobbler is perfect for beginners who don't want to buy a separate strainer.
- The French shaker comes in two pieces and is shaped like the cobbler, but without the integral strainer.
- The Boston shaker is the classic two-piece shaker consisting of a large shaking tin (often metal) and a smaller shaking tin (often glass, and called the pint glass). This shaker is a little trickier to use because you have to make sure you create a seal between the two tins before starting to shake, and it doesn't come with a strainer.

Whichever shaker you choose, pick one you feel comfortable holding and that you can shake and open without releasing a tidal wave of liquor.

HAWTHORN STRAINER

The Hawthorn strainer is a round disc with holes punched in it and a spring running around one edge. This strainer is designed to be a little smaller than most standard cocktail shakers and the spring will fit snugly inside your cocktail shaker's tin, providing a bit of grip and stability when you tip the tin and pour the cocktail out. Some strainers also have 'ears' on each side, which grip to the edge of the shaker and make it even less likely to slip. A Hawthorn strainer is essential if you're using a Boston or French shaker, and it will come in useful if you're using a cobbler shaker to make cocktails with muddled fruit. The handy integral strainers in cobbler shakers can get quickly clogged with fruit pulp, so being able to swap to a Hawthorn strainer gives you more flexibility.

MUDDLER

Muddlers are used to crush soft fruits, extract essential oils from herbs and citrus peel, crack seeds and nuts and even crush ice. When it comes to choosing a muddler the big question is: wood, plastic or steel? Wood is elegant and traditional and can take on most things, but it will need hand washing and drying. Plastic and steel come with the benefit of being dishwasher friendly.

JUICER

If you're making cocktails, you're going to be squeezing plenty of citrus fruits. Some form of lemon juicer will save you a lot of time and mess.

CHOOSE YOUR GLASSWARE

Stocking your bar cart with glasses could see you lining up anything from a few tumblers and highballs to a dozen types of glasses, each one designed for a specific cocktail. When you're picking glasses, think first about what sort of cocktails you are mostly going to make. If you mainly want to perfect your Martini, then a shelf full of flutes and margarita glasses is going to be more ornament than use. There are some specific types of glassware that can form the basis of a solid home bar, and these are my top picks.

Highball and Collins Glasses

Highball glasses are tall and skinny, while Collins glasses are just tall. The difference is minimal, so they can be used interchangeably for long drinks, such as Gin and Tonics and Moscow Mules. When you're picking glasses, avoid the temptation to go for the super-sized option. Unless you want everyone to be plastered before dinner, bigger isn't better. A 350ml (12fl oz) glass is plenty big enough.

Rocks Glasses
Lowball tumblers come in two basic sizes: single rock and double rock (aka the old fashioned glass). Single rock glasses are around 250–300ml (8½–10fl oz) and are ideal for things like Negronis. They comfortably fit a chunk of ice and your drink while still letting you slide a bar spoon in to give everything a spin. Despite the name, double rock glasses aren't double the size. They are more like 300–350ml (10–12fl oz), and while you can serve a whisky and soda in them, they also make great mid-size glasses for drinks with crushed ice, like Juleps, Margaritas and Brambles.

Martini and Coupe Glasses
Fashion has left the classic V-shaped martini glass behind and most modern cocktails are served in a coupe glass. Coupes are a bit smaller than martini glasses, making them more civilized and ensuring that you don't sit with an increasingly tepid vat of gin in front of you. I still have a lot of affection for traditional martini glasses and it's worth looking out for smaller 210ml (7fl oz) ones if, like me, you are nostalgic about 1990s fruit-based Martinis and other cocktail abominations. (Of course, I only use them to serve Vespers and Perfect Manhattans, I promise.) Otherwise, coupes are your go-to glass for cocktails that are served 'up' – meaning stirred or shaken with ice then strained. A set of 170ml (6fl oz) glasses should cover most cocktails.

Wine Glasses and Flutes
Flutes for fizz, of course, and wine glasses for wine, obviously. But wine glasses are also good for Spritzes and Gin and Tonics, if you don't want to add gin copa/balloon glasses to your range of glassware.

All the Right Moves

Mixing drinks is both an art and a science. You can get very nerdy about it and cocktail bars often do, investigating in detail the right level of dilution, the exact temperature for serving, the best techniques for shaking and even the perfect size for ice cubes. As a home cocktail maker, you can get as granular as you like about the science and feel as free to bring as much flair to it as you wish – you could even go the full Tom Cruise in *Cocktail*. Just get the basics of stirring and shaking down first. Once you have that as your foundation, the entire cocktail cart is yours to experiment with.

SHAKEN OR STIRRED?

The fastest way to chill and blend a cocktail is to shake it, but shaking is not always the *best* way to chill and blend it. This is because shaken cocktails can foam up and look cloudy, which isn't always the intended look. A simple rule of thumb is that if your cocktail contains fruit, eggs or dairy, then you shake it. If it's booze and nothing but the booze, you stir it. There are exceptions to this rule (Vesper Martini, I'm looking at you), but broadly speaking it works for most cocktails. And if you're worried about the ice diluting the cocktail: don't be. A little dilution is what you're looking for, especially with stirred cocktails.

HOW TO STIR

Stirred cocktails, like Martinis and Sazeracs, should be clear, crisp and with a silky texture. Start by chilling the mixing glass and the glass you're going to serve your cocktail in. Add enough ice to fill the chilled mixing glass by half to two-thirds, pour in your ingredients and stir with a bar spoon. To hold a bar spoon effectively, place it between your thumb, index and middle fingers with the stem of the spoon resting between your index and middle finger. Place the spoon in the glass so it touches the base, then use your wrist to turn the spoon around the glass. The spoon will begin to spin between your fingers. Keep it moving and stir for around 30 seconds before straining the cocktail into the chilled serving glass.

HOW TO SHAKE

Shaking a cocktail doesn't just chill, blend and dilute it – it also aerates it. Air bubbles are introduced, which gives the drink texture. The first sip of a shaken cocktail should be lively and full of spark. When you're shaking cocktails, pour the ingredients into your shaker and then add ice. How much ice you add depends on how big the ice cubes are. A couple of really big ice cubes or a handful of smaller ice cubes is usually enough. There is a theory that larger ice cubes create smaller bubbles, which gives you a finer texture, but the downside is you have to shake your drink for longer to chill and dilute it. Whatever size ice cubes you choose, once they're added all you need to do is seal your shaker (very important) and then shake well – 15–30 seconds should do it. Strain your cocktail into a chilled glass and serve.

'DRY' AND 'REVERSE DRY' SHAKES

There are two extra ways to shake a cocktail if they have egg white in them: a 'dry' shake and a 'reverse dry' shake. The dry shake involves shaking all the cocktail ingredients together, including the egg white, until it foams, then adding ice and shaking again to chill the cocktail. The reverse dry shake involves shaking all the ingredients apart from the egg white together with ice, then straining out the cocktail, discarding the ice and putting the drink back into the shaker with the egg white. It gets shaken again to foam the egg white, then strained and served. With a reverse dry shake you get larger air bubbles in the egg white, which gives you a fluffier, more dramatic foam. A dry shake gives you smaller bubbles and a smoother foam. It's up to you which you prefer. At the moment I like reverse dry shakes best, but I reserve the right to change my mind in a few years' time and deny that I ever reverse dry shook a thing.

Simple Syrups

A simple syrup is typically a mix of sugar and water boiled together until you get – you've guessed it – a light syrup. With a jar of simple syrup in your fridge, you have that extra something you need to turn a hopeful melange of spirits and fruit juice into actual cocktails. Simple syrup is the most versatile because it's just a liquid sweetener with no flavour of its own, beyond sweetness. But you can also use infused syrups to add flavours, like cardamom or pumpkin spice, or use more interesting sugars for notes of caramel richness (Demerara) or a light floral hint (honey).

SIMPLE SYRUP
Makes about 450ml (16fl oz)
250g (8¾oz) granulated sugar
250ml (8½fl oz) water

Tip the sugar into a saucepan and pour in the water. Set the pan on a medium-high heat and bring to the boil, without stirring. Once boiling, set your timer for 2 minutes. After 2 minutes, take the pan off the heat and let the syrup cool. Transfer to a sterilized jar or tub, seal and store in the fridge for up to 1 month.

DEMERARA SYRUP
Makes about 450ml (16fl oz)
250g (8¾oz) Demerara (raw) sugar
250ml (8½fl oz) water

Tip the sugar into a saucepan and pour in the water. Set the pan on a medium-high heat and bring to the boil, without stirring. Once the pan is boiling, set your timer for 2 minutes. After 2 minutes, take the pan off the heat and let the syrup cool. Transfer to a sterilized jar or tub, seal and store in the fridge for up to 1 month.

HONEY SYRUP
Makes about 450ml (16fl oz)
250ml (8½fl oz) water
250g (8¾oz) honey

Pour the water and honey into a pan and set it on a medium-high heat. Bring to the boil, without stirring. Once boiling, set your timer for 2 minutes.

After 2 minutes, take the pan off the heat and let the syrup cool in the pan. Transfer the syrup to a sterilized jar or tub, seal and store in the fridge for up to 1 month.

LEMON AND HONEY SYRUP
Makes about 450ml (16fl oz)
2 large lemons
250g (8¾oz) honey

Use a vegetable peeler to peel the zest from both lemons, leaving as much white pith behind as possible, and place it in a pan. Juice the lemons into a measuring jug, then top up with water until you have 250ml (8½fl oz) liquid. Pour the honey and the diluted lemon juice into the pan with the lemon peel. Set the pan on a medium-high heat and bring to the boil, without stirring. Once boiling, set your timer for 2 minutes. After 2 minutes, take the pan off the heat and let the syrup cool in the pan. Strain the syrup through a fine-mesh sieve and discard the lemon zest. Transfer the syrup to a sterilized jar or tub, seal and store in the fridge for up to 2 weeks.

HONEY AND GINGER SYRUP
Makes about 450ml (16fl oz)
250ml (8½fl oz) water
250g (8¾oz) honey
25g (1oz) fresh ginger, peeled and finely sliced

Pour the water and honey into a pan and set it on a medium-high heat. Bring to the boil, without stirring. Once boiling, add the ginger then set your timer for 2 minutes and let the syrup boil. After 2 minutes, take the pan off the heat and let the syrup cool in the pan. Strain the cooled syrup through a fine-mesh sieve into a jug and discard the ginger. Transfer the syrup to a sterilized jar or tub, seal and store in the fridge for up to 2 weeks.

PUMPKIN SPICE SYRUP
Makes about 450ml (16fl oz)
250g (8¾oz) soft dark brown sugar
250ml (8½fl oz) water
60g (2oz) pumpkin purée
1 tsp ground cinnamon
½ tsp ground ginger
4 whole cloves
½ nutmeg
1 tsp vanilla bean paste or vanilla extract

Tip the sugar into a saucepan and pour in the water. Set the pan on a medium-high heat and bring to the boil, without stirring. Once boiling, turn the heat down a little and add the pumpkin purée, the cinnamon, ginger, cloves and grate in half a nutmeg. Add the vanilla paste or extract. Gently simmer for 10 minutes, stirring occasionally. After 10 minutes, take the pan off the heat and let the syrup cool. Strain the cooled syrup through a fine-mesh sieve into a jug and discard the spices and pumpkin. Transfer the syrup to a sterilized jar or tub, seal and store in the fridge for up to 2 weeks.

BEETROOT SYRUP

Makes about 450ml (16fl oz)

200g (7oz) beetroot, peeled and chopped
250g (8¾oz) granulated sugar
250ml (8½fl oz) water

Tip the beetroot into a saucepan. Add the sugar and pour in the water. Set the pan on a medium-high heat and bring to the boil, without stirring. Once boiling, pop a lid on the pan and turn the heat down. Gently simmer for

30 minutes. Take the pan off the heat and let it cool. Strain the cooled syrup through a fine-mesh sieve into a jug and discard the beetroot. Transfer the syrup to a sterilized jar or tub, seal and store in the fridge for up to 2 weeks.

CARDAMOM SYRUP

Makes about 450ml (16fl oz)

20g (¾oz) green cardamom pods
250g (8¾oz) granulated sugar
250ml (8½fl oz) water

Tip the cardamom pods into a saucepan and lightly bash them with a muddler, a pestle or the end of a rolling pin to just open them up a little. Tip the sugar into the saucepan and pour in the water. Set the pan on a medium-high heat and bring to the boil, without stirring. Once boiling, set your timer for 2 minutes. After 2 minutes, take the pan off the heat and let the syrup cool. Strain the cooled syrup through a fine-mesh sieve into a jug and discard the cardamom pods. Transfer the syrup to a sterilized jar or tub, seal and store in the fridge for up to 1 month.

MULLED WINE SPICE SYRUP

Makes about 450ml (16fl oz)
250g (8¾oz) granulated sugar
250ml (8½fl oz) water
1 orange, quartered
25g (1oz) fresh ginger, peeled
  and thickly sliced
8 whole cloves
2 cinnamon sticks
¼ nutmeg

Tip the sugar into the saucepan and pour in the water. Add the orange and ginger to the pan. Drop in the cloves and cinnamon sticks. Grate in one-quarter of a nutmeg.

Set the pan on a medium-high heat and bring to the boil, without stirring. Once boiling, set your timer for 2 minutes. After 2 minutes, take the pan off the heat and let the syrup cool. Strain the cooled syrup through a fine-mesh sieve into a jug and discard the spices, oranges and ginger. Transfer the syrup to a sterilized jar or tub, seal and store in the fridge for up to 1 month.

Make Your Own Warming Winter Liqueurs

Autumn (fall) and winter are great preserving seasons. Whether it's hedgerow berries or crates of citrus fruits, the cooler months provide plenty of ingredients for keen cocktail makers who want to build their own bar of D-I-Y liqueurs. It's very easy and normally takes just a few minutes. The main thing to remember when you're making liqueurs and infusions is to always use a good-quality base spirit. Cheaper spirits tend to be a bit rough around the edges, and that normally means ladling more sugar into the liqueur to cover up the firewater flavours. A solid, mid-market gin, vodka, whisky or brandy will give you crisper, better-balanced results.

SLOE GIN

Makes about 900ml (1½ pints)

400g (14oz) sloes
2 almonds
125g (4½oz) caster (superfine)
  sugar
700ml (1¼ pints) London dry gin

Prepare your sloes by pricking them all over with a sterilized needle or putting them in a freezerproof tub or bag and freezing them for 48 hours to crack them. Tip the sloes into a 1½ litre (2.65 pint) sterilized jar. Lightly crush the almonds and add them to the jar with the sugar. Pour in the gin. Seal the jar and leave it to steep somewhere dark and dry for 3–12 months. Shake the jar every few days during the first couple of weeks to help dissolve the sugar. After at least 3 months, strain the gin through a sieve and taste it. If it's not sweet enough, stir in a little cooled Simple Syrup (see page 12) until it's sweet enough. Pour back into the jar or a sterilized bottle to store.

How to Serve

Sloe Gin is great served on the rocks or chill it and serve straight up with a cheeseboard after a meal. Add a splash to Champagne to make a Sloe Royale, or pour a generous measure into a highball glass, add ice and top up with bitter lemon.

DAMSON VODKA

Makes about 900ml (1½ pints)

400g (14oz) damsons
125g (4½oz) caster (superfine)
  sugar
700ml (1¼ pints) vodka

Prepare your damsons by pricking them all over with a sterilized needle or putting them in a freezerproof tub or bag and freezing them for 48 hours to crack them. Tip the damsons into a 1½ litre (2.65 pint) sterilized jar and add the sugar. Pour in the vodka. Seal the jar and leave it to steep somewhere dark and dry for 3–12 months. Shake the jar every few days during the first couple of weeks to help dissolve the sugar. After at least 3 months, strain the vodka through a sieve and taste it. If it's not sweet enough, stir in a little cooled Simple Syrup (see page 12) until it's sweet enough. Pour back into the jar or a sterilized bottle and store.

How to Serve

Like Sloe Gin, Damson Vodka is good on the rocks or chilled and served straight up. For a long drink, serve in a highball glass over ice, topped up with soda water (club soda) and a squeeze of lime juice.

RHUBARB VODKA

Makes about 900ml (1½ pints)
400g (14oz) rhubarb
250g (8¾oz) caster
    (superfine) sugar
2 tbsp fresh lemon juice
700ml (1¼ pints) vodka

Wash and trim the rhubarb and chop it into 2cm (¾in) chunks. Scoop into a sterilized 1½ litre (2.65 pint) jar. Add the sugar and lemon juice. Seal the jar and give it a good shake. Let the rhubarb sit in the sugar for 24 hours – this will draw the juices out of the rhubarb. After 24 hours, pour in the vodka, seal the jar again and leave to steep somewhere dark and dry for 2 weeks. After 2 weeks, strain the vodka through a sieve. Discard the rhubarb and pour the vodka back into the jar or a sterilized bottle and store.

How to Serve

Add tonic water to a shot of Rhubarb Vodka over ice for a sherbetty fizz, or try mixing it with ginger beer and a squeeze of lime juice to make a Rhubarb Mule.

BLACKBERRY BRANDY

Makes about 900ml (1½ pints)
250g (8¾oz) blackberries
100g (3½oz) caster (superfine)
    sugar
A strip of lime zest or a bay
    leaf (optional)
700ml (1¼ pints) brandy

Tip the blackberries and sugar into a 1 litre (1.7 pint) sterilized jar. If you're using the lime zest, peel a strip of zest from a lime and scrape off as much of the white pith as possible. Drop the lime zest or bay leaf into the jar (or leave them out entirely), seal the jar and give it a good shake to crush the blackberries. Pour in the brandy. Seal the jar again and leave it to steep somewhere dark and dry for 1–2 weeks. Shake the jar every day to help dissolve the sugar. After 1–2 weeks, strain it through a sieve. Discard the blackberries and lime zest/bay leaf and pour

17

the brandy back into the jar or into a sterilized bottle to store.

How to Serve
Straight up or on the rocks, if you prefer your Blackberry Brandy chilled. Blackberry Brandy also makes a deliciously autumnal Sidecar: shake 45ml (1½fl oz) with 30ml (1fl oz) Cointreau, 15ml (½fl oz) lemon juice and plenty of ice, then strain into a chilled coupe glass and serve with blackberries or an orange twist to garnish.

CLEMENTINE BOURBON
Makes about 900ml (1½ pints)
2–3 clementines
700ml (1¼ pints) bourbon

Quarter the clementines, keeping the skin on, and add them to a sterilized 1½ litre (2.65 pint) jar. Add the bourbon, seal the jar and leave it to steep somewhere dark and dry for 1–2 weeks. After 1 week, taste the bourbon and if you would like a more citrusy flavour, leave the bourbon to infuse for another week. After 2 weeks, strain through a sieve. Discard the clementines and pour the bourbon

back into the jar or into a sterilised bottle and store.

How to Serve
Clementine Bourbon makes a great Old Fashioned. Stir 60ml (2fl oz) Clementine Bourbon with 1 teaspoon Demerara Syrup (see page 12) and 2 dashes of Peychauds bitters over ice and serve with an orange twist.

STERILIZING JARS AND BOTTLES

To sterilize glass jars and bottles, preheat your oven to 160°C/325°F/140°C fan/ Gas mark 3. Wash the jars and/or bottles in hot, soapy water (including the lids) then rinse and place on a baking tray. Slide into the oven and heat for around 15 minutes. Take them out of the oven, add the liqueur ingredients and seal. Remember the jars are hot (I have made this mistake before, as my blistered and scarred fingers can attest), so leave them to cool before you start shaking them.

The Recipes

Note: All recipes serve 1, unless otherwise stated

Spiked Apple Punch

The first time I went to New York it was October, and we landed a few days before Halloween. We'd come prepared, with costumes in our suitcases so we could join the parade, and thank goodness we did. On the day, every costume shop in Manhattan had a line of would-be wizards, ghosts and vampires waiting outside it. We strolled past them, amazed and impressed, starting to understand just how big our Halloween night out was going to be. In the farmers' market a tiny dog in a witch's hat and cloak ran up to us to be petted (tricky with the hat on) while we were buying cups of mulled apple juice (cider) spiced with cinnamon and cloves. We never did make the parade – too busy bar-hopping with a motley collection of ghouls and werewolves. But in memory of that holiday I've made a boozy version of that mulled apple drink, pepped up with dark rum and a dash of Angostura bitters.

Serves 4–6

1 orange
1 lemon
8 whole cloves
1 cinnamon stick
750ml (1.3 pints) cloudy apple juice
120ml (4fl oz) dark rum
Angostura bitters, to serve

INSTRUCTIONS

Quarter the orange and lemon and push a clove into each quarter. Place the fruit in a large pan and drop in the cinnamon stick. Pour in the apple juice and dark rum. Set the pan on a medium heat and warm until the pan is steaming hot. Turn the heat down to low, pop on a lid and gently warm for 10 minutes to mingle the flavours. Ladle the punch into heatproof mugs or glasses. Add a dash of Angostura bitters to each glass and serve.

Falling Leaves

Towards the end of autumn (fall) the paths in my local park are carpeted with leaves. A thread of scarlet, gold and amber winds past the bare-branched trees, up the hill, where I can stand and watch the sun set over London's high-rises. The weather starts to get cold as the leaves fall from the trees and, coming home from the park, I like to snuggle up on the sofa with a cocktail in a chunky glass tumbler, full of ice and rich flavours. This chocolaty, change-of-season cocktail fits the bill perfectly.

45ml (1½fl oz) rye whisky
22ml (¾fl oz) Amaro Averna
22ml (¾fl oz) crème de figue
2 dashes of chocolate bitters
Orange slice, to garnish

INSTRUCTIONS

Pour the whisky, Amaro and crème de figue into a single rock glass filled with ice. Add 2 dashes of chocolate bitters and stir well to chill. Drop in a slice of orange to garnish and serve.

Pumpkin Spiced Espresso Martini

Pumpkin spice season arrives on the first of September (and not before, in spite of what some coffee chains try to tell you) and it marks the end of summer, and the beginning of autumn (fall). It means goodbye flip-flops, hello cosy jumpers and hiking boots. The weather doesn't always play ball, so sometimes you have to find a more refreshing, icier version of the classic pumpkin spice latte, and I think this espresso martini is it. The original Espresso Martini was invented in London in the early 1980s by Dick Bradsell, bartender at the time in the Soho Brasserie. This autumnal twist adds a healthy dash of pumpkin spice to the original mix of vodka, coffee liqueur and espresso. To get the famous creamy layer of foam on top of your Espresso Martini, make sure the espresso is freshly made and give it a really good shake when you're mixing it.

22ml (¾fl oz) Pumpkin Spice Syrup (see page 13)
45ml (1½fl oz) vanilla vodka
35ml (1¼fl oz) freshly made espresso
22ml (¾fl oz) Kahlua
Freshly grated nutmeg, to garnish

INSTRUCTIONS
Make the Pumpkin Spice Syrup following the recipe on page 13. Put a martini glass into the freezer for at least 30 minutes, or fill it with ice and let it chill for a few minutes. Pour all the ingredients into a shaker, add a handful of ice and then give it a really good shake for around 30 seconds or so. Strain into the chilled glass and serve dusted with a little freshly grated nutmeg.

Old Fashioned Hot Toddy

The Old Fashioned is the original cocktail. The drink every 19th-century American bartender could mix. Over time this deceptively simple mix of whisky, Angostura bitters and sugar has fallen in and out of fashion, but bartenders and barflies always end up coming back to it. For the colder months, rather than serve it iced, try turning it into a Hot Toddy. A spoonful of Honey Syrup stands in for the sugar cube, giving the toddy a mellow sweetness. Fresh orange helps bring out the zestier elements in the Angostura bitters, while the malted richness of the whisky is sure to warm you up.

1 tbsp Honey Syrup (see page 12)
50ml (1¾fl oz) rye whisky
1 slice of orange
Boiling water, to top up
2 dashes of Angostura bitters

INSTRUCTIONS
Make the Honey Syrup following the recipe on page 12. When you're ready to make the toddy, pour the whisky into a mug or heatproof glass and add 1 tablespoon of the syrup. Drop in the orange slice. Top up the mug with around 100–150ml (3½–5¼fl oz) boiling water and stir to dissolve the syrup. Add 2 dashes of Angostura bitters. Taste and add a little more syrup if you think it needs it, then serve.

San Francisco

In 1937 the *Café Royal Cocktail Book* was published with a limited run of just 25 copies. The author was William J. Tarling, then President of the United Kingdom Bartenders' Guild, who'd studied over 4,000 cocktail recipes in order to put together a book of modern cocktails for the discerning host. It's a fascinating read and there is a facsimile edition of it online for cocktail fans that want to geek out on early 20th-century cocktail history. One of the most delicious cocktails in the book is the San Francisco. Tarling doesn't explain why this variation on a sweet Martini is named after the Golden City. Perhaps a San Franciscan sent him the recipe, or maybe a romantic London bartender named this plummy mix of sloe gin and vermouth after his dream holiday destination. We'll never know. But, on a warm evening, we can sit with an icy San Francisco and imagine ourselves in California, watching the fog roll in across the bay.

30ml (1fl oz) sloe gin
30ml (1fl oz) dry vermouth
30ml (1fl oz) sweet vermouth
1 dash of Old Fashion Aromatic Bitters (if you don't
    have these, then Angostura or Jerry Thomas
    bitters will work just as well)
1 dash of orange bitters
Maraschino cherry, to garnish

INSTRUCTIONS
Put a small coupe glass into the freezer for at least 30 minutes, or fill it with ice and leave it to chill for a few minutes. Pour the sloe gin and the two vermouths into a shaker and add 1 dash each of the bitters. Add a couple of ice cubes and give it a really good shake to chill. Strain into the chilled glass and serve, garnished with a maraschino cherry.

Charlie Chaplin

Add some Old Hollywood glamour to autumnal evenings with this 1920s cocktail named after the legendary silent movie actor. It was invented at the Waldorf Astoria in New York, just months before Prohibition began. The original recipe was a 1:1:1 mix of sloe gin, lime juice and apricot brandy, making it a fairly sweet and lethally strong concoction. The drink has gone through a few evolutions since then and this version is based on the one served at Balthazar in London's Covent Garden. They have added damson vodka to the mix, upping the plummy flavours and helping to balance the sweetness with an extra bite of booze.

15ml (½fl oz) sloe gin (shop-bought or homemade,
    see page 16)
15ml (½fl oz) Damson Vodka (see page 16)
15ml (½fl oz) apricot brandy
22ml (¾fl oz) fresh lime juice
8ml (¼fl oz) Simple Syrup (see page 12)

INSTRUCTIONS
Make the Simple Syrup following the recipe on page 12. Put a small coupe glass into the freezer for at least 30 minutes, or fill it with ice and let it chill for a few minutes. Put all the ingredients into a shaker, then add a handful of ice and give it a really good shake. Strain into the chilled glass and serve.

Smashed Pumpkin

Every October my neighbourhood is transformed from a quiet, sedate little suburb made of red brick and flowerbeds into Halloween Town – the spookiest, scariest spot on the planet. Sticky white spiderwebs swallow up the hedges and, if you're brave and look closely, you'll see the beady eyes and hairy legs of the giant spiders and creepy crawlies that lurk beneath the leaves. Black cats and bats peep out of windows while vampires and ghosts hide behind fences and garden gates. And on every doorstep there is a leering Jack O'Lantern, grinning its tombstone grin and watching the night with flickering yellow eyes. The lanterns are there to guard the houses from evil spirits – or maybe they welcome them in. This Halloween cocktail tips its hat to the Pumpkin King and all the mysterious things that go bump in the night.

22ml (¾fl oz) Pumpkin Spice Syrup (see page 13)
60ml (2fl oz) bourbon
30ml (1fl oz) fresh lemon juice
2 dashes of orange bitters
15ml (½fl oz) egg white

INSTRUCTIONS

Make the Pumpkin Spice Syrup following the recipe on page 13. Put a coupe glass into the freezer for at least 30 minutes, or fill it with ice and let it chill for a few minutes. Pour the syrup, bourbon and lemon juice into a cocktail shaker and add a handful of ice. Add 2 dashes of orange bitters. Shake for 30 seconds to chill, then strain the cocktail out into a clean glass (not the coupe), discard the ice and add the cocktail mix back to the shaker. Pour in the egg white. Shake again for 30 seconds. Strain into the chilled glass and serve.

Cardamom and Whisky Cobbler

A cobbler is loosely defined as a drink made with a spirit or fortified wine shaken with fruit and a little syrup and served over crushed ice. The name is said to have come from the little cobbles of ice – crushed ice being a new thing in the 1830s, when the first cobblers made their way into bars. There are two essentials you can't leave off your cobbler: an extravagant garnish, and straws. The garnish is just for fun, but fun is key to a good cocktail. The straws stop you burying your nose in crushed ice every time you take a sip. This cobbler is light and frothy, with a warming heat from the mix of whisky, cognac and cardamom. If you want to serve it at a party – and cobblers make great party drinks – then crush plenty of pineapple beforehand and just add a few spoonfuls to your shaker every time you mix a drink.

22ml (¾fl oz) Cardamom Syrup (see page 14)
25g (1oz) fresh pineapple (or use tinned in juice if preferred)
60ml (2fl oz) blended Scotch whisky
15ml (½fl oz) Cognac
15ml (½fl oz) fresh lime juice
Pineapple wedge and mint sprigs, to garnish

INSTRUCTIONS

Make the Cardamom Syrup following the recipe on page 14. Chop the fresh pineapple and tip it into a shaker. Use a muddler, a pestle or the end of a rolling pin to muddle it (crush it), then pour in the prepared syrup, whisky, Cognac and lime juice. Add a handful of ice and give it a really good shake. Fill a wine glass or goblet with crushed ice and strain in the whisky cobbler. Give the drink a good stir to churn it with the crushed ice, then garnish with a wedge of fresh pineapple and a couple of sprigs of mint to serve.

Chai Spiced Mulled Cider

One upside to the arrival of longer, darker nights is the promise of bonfires and fireworks. Whether it's Diwali, Christmas or New Year, there is always at least one firework show to go to and one bonfire to be lit. Of course, standing outside in winter watching fireworks fizz across the sky means finding ways to keep warm. A hat, gloves and a glass of mulled cider are the perfect combination for me. This mulled cider is flavoured with a mix of spices used in chai masala. They pair wonderfully with the fruity apple flavours in cider, and toasting them for a few minutes helps to bring out their aroma.

Serves 8

150ml (5¼fl oz) Demerara Syrup (see page 12)
1 cinnamon stick
6 whole cloves
1 star anise
1 tsp coriander seeds
6 cardamom pods

1 tsp black peppercorns
1.5 litres (2⅔ pints) medium dry cider
Juice of 1 lemon
4cm (1½in) chunk of fresh ginger
1 apple, cored and sliced

INSTRUCTIONS

Make the Demerara Syrup following the recipe on page 12. Put a large pan on a medium heat and add the cinnamon stick, cloves, star anise, coriander seeds, cardamom pods and peppercorns to the pan. Toast, stirring, for 2–3 minutes until the spices smell aromatic. Pour in the cider, lemon juice and syrup. Slice the ginger and add it to the pan. Warm until the cider is steaming hot. Turn the heat down to low, cover with a lid and gently warm for 15 minutes to mingle the flavours. Drop the apple slices into heatproof glasses or mugs. Ladle in the mulled cider, leaving the spices in the pan, and serve.

Red Wine Hot Chocolate

Red wine and dark chocolate are natural flavour mates, so although a red-wine-infused hot chocolate might sound a bit crazy, it actually makes perfect sense. Pick a fruity, jammy red wine that isn't too heavy on the tannins and use a good-quality chocolate to make sure the flavours blend beautifully. This is a great drink for sipping in the garden on an autumn afternoon, when it's a little too chilly for cold drinks, and a little too early for a full glass of wine.

1 tsp cocoa powder
25g (1oz) 70% cocoa dark chocolate, broken into pieces
½ tsp vanilla bean paste or vanilla extract
150ml (5¼fl oz) full-fat milk
50ml (1¾fl oz) red wine, such as Merlot or Pinot Noir
Marshmallows, to serve

INSTRUCTIONS

Tip the cocoa powder into a small pan and add the chocolate. Add the vanilla paste or extract, milk and red wine. Set the pan on a medium heat and warm, whisking, until the chocolate has melted and everything is smoothly combined and just steaming hot. Pour the hot chocolate into a mug or heatproof wine glass and top with marshmallows.

Baileys Latte

My sister Cara makes the best brunch. Not only does she make perfect fluffy pancakes that come served in a stack with crisp rashers of bacon and a drizzle of maple syrup, she is also a dab hand at making Baileys Lattes. Decadent, indulgent and a little outrageous, drinking a Baileys Latte is like getting a reassuring hug from a drag queen – cosy but also a little wicked. It's a delicious duvet of a drink that wraps you up in a tipsy mix of caffeine, cream and Irish whiskey. It's not too boozy, which is what makes it great for brunch. But drink more than two and you may find that, in spite of the coffee, a little nap becomes necessary.

200ml (7fl oz) full-fat milk
35ml (1¼fl oz) freshly made espresso
50ml (1¾fl oz) Baileys Irish Cream Liqueur
Cocoa powder or finely grated dark chocolate, whipped (heavy)
    cream (or squirty cream), to serve (optional)

INSTRUCTIONS
Pour the milk into a pan and warm for a few minutes, whisking constantly to create a fine layer of foam on the top of the milk. When the milk is steaming hot but not boiling, take it off the heat. Pour a large shot of fresh espresso into a heatproof glass or mug, then pour in the Baileys. Top up with the milk and spoon over any foam left in the pan. You can dust over a little cocoa powder or finely grated dark chocolate, or go mad and top it with cream and chocolate.

Boulevardier

Inject a little 1920s glamour into your autumn by mixing yourself a Boulevardier. It was created by Harry McElhone at Harry's New York Bar in Paris to honour the American expat and wealthy man-about-town Erskine Gwynne. Erskine edited a magazine called *The Boulevardier*, which is where the drink got its name. It's a kissing cousin to the Negroni, with bourbon subbed in for the gin. The bourbon gives the drink an oaky richness that makes it a smoother sip, perfect for lingering over as the nights get longer and the conversations more interesting. For parties, scale the recipe up and stir together in a jug with ice. It makes a great welcome drink for Thanksgiving gatherings and winter dinner parties.

35ml (1¼fl oz) bourbon
22ml (¾fl oz) sweet vermouth
22ml (¾fl oz) Campari
Orange twist, to serve

INSTRUCTIONS
Fill a tumbler with ice and pour in the bourbon, sweet vermouth and Campari. Stir well to chill, then garnish with an orange twist to serve.

Sparkling Cranberry Punch

A punch bowl is always a delight at parties. They look so grand and impressive, and the joy of them is that guests can ladle out their own drinks so hosts can enjoy their party rather than run around topping up glasses. For holiday parties and Thanksgiving gatherings this year, put a punch bowl on the table and fill it with this fizzy pink drink inspired by the 1990s cocktail classic, the Sea Breeze. There's a hefty hit of vodka in it and Prosecco is one of the mixers, so it is best served in small punch cups to encourage dainty sipping rather than glugging. The cranberry and grapefruit juice add a fruity crispness to the drink, as well as a festive dash of colour.

Serves 12–14

400ml (14fl oz) vodka
700ml (1¼ pints) cranberry juice
700ml (1¼ pints) pink grapefruit juice
12–14 dashes of Peychauds bitters
1½ litres (2.65 pints) chilled Prosecco Brut
Frozen cranberries and lime wedges, to serve

INSTRUCTIONS

In a large mixing glass or jug, mix together the vodka, cranberry juice and pink grapefruit juice. Add the Peychauds bitters and stir. Cover and chill in the fridge until you're ready to serve the punch. When you're ready to start serving drinks, add a few handfuls of ice to a large punch bowl or a couple of serving jugs and drop in frozen cranberries and wedges of lime. Pour in the vodka-cranberry mix. Top up with chilled Prosecco and briefly stir. Ladle or pour into small glasses with extra ice.

Bandon Bronco

This wintry twist on a Moscow Mule adds tart cranberry juice to the mix, giving the drink a festive hint of pink and a fruity flavour that marries up nicely with the lime and ginger. The cranberry juice also explains the drink's name. Bandon is the capital of cranberries in Oregon, and as the drink still kicks like a mule, it had to be a Bandon Bronco. If you want to make it ahead for a holiday party, mix the vodka, cranberry and lime juice together and chill them till you're ready to make up pitchers of the drink, topped up with ginger beer.

Serves 6

250ml (8½fl oz) vodka
450ml (16fl oz) cranberry juice
150ml (5½fl oz) fresh lime juice
450ml (16fl oz) ginger beer
Lime wedges, to serve

Instructions

Half-fill a large mixing glass with ice and pour in the vodka, cranberry and lime juices and give it a good stir to mix. Fill 6 Collins glasses or copper mugs with ice and pour in the Bandon Bronco mix. Top up with the ginger beer, gently stir and serve each garnished with a lime wedge.

Frozen Fig Daiquiri

Made famous by the Floridita Bar in Havana, Frozen Daiquiris feel like a summer drink, but when autumn has such great fresh fruit it seems a shame not to get the kitchen blender out and make up a batch of harvest cocktails. Figs make a sherbet-like Daiquiri, pale pink and tangy. The basic mix of rum, lime juice and Simple Syrup can also be teamed with your favourite autumn (fall) fruits, such as plums, peaches, nectarines and blackberries to make an adults-only spiked slushy.

2–3 plump, ripe figs
60ml (2fl oz) white rum
30ml (1fl oz) fresh lime juice
15ml (½fl oz) Simple Syrup (see page 12)

INSTRUCTIONS

Make the Simple Syrup following the recipe on page 12.
Put a large martini or coupe glass into the freezer for at least 30 minutes, or fill it with ice and let it chill for a few minutes. Trim the woody stems off the figs and roughly chop the figs. Pop them in a blender with a handful of ice. Pour in the rum, lime juice and syrup and blitz to make a slushy mixture. Taste and add a little more lime juice or syrup if you think it needs it, then pour the Frozen Daiquiri into the chilled glass and serve.

Apple Brandy Sour

Nothing says autumn (fall) like apples. Crisp, crunchy, sweet and juicy, apples are the stuff of early autumn picnics, packed in a basket with cheese sandwiches and salted snacks. They're warming pies and crumbles, served with scoops of vanilla ice cream and hot lakes of custard. Apples are cold-weather breakfasts, grated and stirred with oats, raisins and honey to make porridge. An autumn without apples is no autumn at all and if, for some reason, your fruit bowl remains apple-free, then make this Apple Brandy Sour. It tastes like cider on steroids and will bring a rosy glow to your (no doubt apple-y) cheeks.

60ml (2fl oz) apple brandy
30ml (1fl oz) fresh lemon juice
22ml (¾fl oz) maple syrup
3 dashes of Angostura bitters
15ml (½fl oz) egg white
Maraschino cherry, to garnish

INSTRUCTIONS

Put a coupe glass into the freezer for at least 30 minutes, or fill it with ice and leave it to chill for a few minutes. Pour the apple brandy, lemon juice and maple syrup into a cocktail shaker and add a handful of ice. Add 3 dashes of Angostura bitters. Shake well to chill, then strain the cocktail into a clean glass (not the coupe), discard the ice and add the cocktail mix back to the shaker. Pour in the egg white. Shake again for 30 seconds or so. Drop a maraschino cherry into the chilled glass, then strain in the Apple Brandy Sour and serve.

Hot Ale Flip

The oldest cocktail in the world? Probably. The earliest mention of a Flip is in William Congreve's 17th-century play *Love for Love*, in which a cheerful troop of seamen prance on stage and proclaim: 'We're merry folks, we sailors: we han't much to care for. Thus we live at sea; eat biscuit, and drink flip.' Flips – made with brandy, sugar and ale, and stirred with a hot poker until the beer sizzles and the sugar caramelizes – were the drink of choice for sailors and other rough folk. Those sailors took the Flip to America, where colonial tavern-keepers added eggs and turned it into a drink you'd welcome after a long, cold journey in a rackety old coach. This version is light, zesty and warming.

2 tbsp lemon juice
1 tbsp Demerara (raw) sugar
330ml (11½fl oz) brown ale

22ml (¾fl oz) dark rum
1 small egg
Freshly grated nutmeg, to serve

INSTRUCTIONS
Pour the lemon juice into a medium pan and add the sugar and ale. Place on a medium heat and gently warm, stirring occasionally, until the sugar has dissolved and the beer is starting to steam. Pour the rum into a separate medium or large pan and whisk in the egg. Add a few spoonfuls of the warm beer (not too much or it will scramble the egg) and whisk until smoothly combined. Add a few more spoonfuls of warm beer and whisk again. Repeat, adding another tablespoon of beer, then add the remaining beer. Doing this slowly stops the egg cooking and making a beery omelette. Once combined, pour back into the original pan, then pour it back and forth 3–4 times, until the ale is foamy and the colour of tea. Alternatively, keep it in one pan and give it a good whisk until foamy. Pour into a heatproof beer glass or jug. Grate a little nutmeg over the top before serving.

Spiked Mexican Chocolate Caliente

A cup of Mexican hot chocolate, gently spiced with cinnamon and whisked until frothy, is a delicious way to warm up when the weather starts to turn chilly. In Mexico, hot chocolate is made with *chocolate de mesa*, a slightly grainy mix of cacao, sugar and cinnamon sold in tablets, ready for chopping and melting with milk. If you can get hold of it then you can leave the cinnamon and vanilla out of this recipe and just make it with the solid drinking chocolate, milk and mezcal. If not, then this indulgent version of chocolate caliente made with cocoa-heavy dark chocolate and a touch of spice will taste just as good, especially with an earthy shot of mezcal added just before serving.

180ml (6fl oz) full-fat milk
½ cinnamon stick
½ tsp vanilla bean paste or vanilla extract
50g (1¾oz) 70% cocoa dark chocolate,
    roughly chopped
30ml (1fl oz) mezcal

INSTRUCTIONS

Pour the milk into a small pan and add the cinnamon stick, vanilla paste or extract and chocolate. Set the pan on a medium heat and gently warm, stirring, until the chocolate has melted and is smoothly combined. Take the pan off the heat, fish out the cinnamon stick and whisk the hot chocolate until it's nice and frothy. Pour the mezcal into a heatproof mug and pour in the hot chocolate. Serve straight away.

55

Black Tea Hot Toddy

You could almost believe that this toddy is just a cup of tea, if it wasn't so very warming. This brandy-spiked drink is a smoother sip than the traditional, whisky-based Hot Toddy, thanks to the aromatic flavour of the tea. Use a good-quality tea for this drink, and if English breakfast isn't your brew of choice then swap in floral Earl Grey or smoky Assam. (Although, if you're using Assam I'd be tempted to swap the brandy for whisky and before you know it you're inventing your own tea-based cocktails.)

150ml (5¼fl oz) hot English breakfast tea
1 slice of lemon
2 whole cloves
35ml (1¼fl oz) brandy
1 tbsp lemon juice
1 tbsp honey
1 cinnamon stick

INSTRUCTIONS

Brew the tea for 1–2 minutes – this toddy is best made with a lighter brew than your standard breakfast drink, but steep the tea for longer if you like it tannin-heavy. Stud the slice of lemon with the whole cloves. Pour the brandy into a mug or heatproof glass and add the lemon juice and honey. Drop in the lemon slice and cinnamon stick. Top up the mug with the hot tea and stir to dissolve the honey. Serve straight away.

Death by Chocolate

The unlikeliest of drinks, this cocktail ended up in this book by way of two rock stars and a podcast. I first heard about it on the *Off Menu* podcast, where guests choose their perfect three-course meal and a drink to go with it. Welsh singer Cerys Matthews picked Death by Chocolate as her drink. She'd been told about it by Ian Brown, lead singer of 1990s Brit band the Stone Roses, and she promised the podcast listeners that if they mixed vodka and Tia Maria with Guinness they'd end up with half a pint of boozy liquid chocolate. I had to try it, and it turned out Cerys was right. It really does taste like chocolate – incredibly dangerous chocolate that could lead to a sore head in the morning, but chocolate nonetheless. If you're a chocolate-orange fan, swap the vodka for Cointreau and you can luxuriate in boozy chocolate-orange heaven.

22ml (¾fl oz) vodka
22ml (¾fl oz) Tia Maria
250ml (8½fl oz) Guinness Original Stout Beer, chilled

INSTRUCTIONS
Pour the vodka and Tia Maria into a half pint glass, then top up with chilled Guinness to serve.

Canalezo

In the Andean highlands of Ecuador the best way to warm up on a cool evening is with a Canalezo. The drink's name is derived from *canela* – the Spanish word for cinnamon, which is the main ingredient in this richly aromatic brew. You make it by simmering cinnamon sticks with brown sugar and lime juice until you have an amber-hued liquid headily full of sweet spice. Traditionally, you add the hot cinnamon water to shots of aguardiente, a South American sugar cane spirit. If that's not available in your local store, then swap in white rum or cachaça.

Serves 4

4 cinnamon sticks
75g (2½oz) soft dark brown sugar
Juice of 2 limes
120ml (4fl oz) aguardiente, white rum or cachaça

Instructions

Pour 500ml (17fl oz) water into a pan and add the cinnamon sticks, dark brown sugar and lime juice. Cover the pan with a lid, set on a medium-high heat and bring to the boil. Once the water is boiling, turn the heat down to low and gently simmer for 40 minutes. Pour 30ml (1fl oz) aguardiente, white rum or cachaça into 4 heatproof glasses or mugs, then strain in the hot cinnamon water and serve.

Tokyo Toddy

A toddy is typically made with a spirit stirred with hot water and sweetened, but you don't always have to use water as the mixer. This toddy takes its inspiration from Japan and uses a warm sake mixed with the marmalade sweetness of Mandarine Napoleon to create a full-flavoured drink packed with malt and caramel that would be delicious paired with sushi, sashimi or light tofu dishes. When you're choosing a sake to make this toddy, pick a honjozo sake. Honjozo sakes tend to be lighter and drier than other sakes, which means they don't become overly sweet when you start adding orange liqueur, sugar and spice to them.

150ml (5¼fl oz) honjozo sake
30ml (1fl oz) Mandarine Napoleon Liqueur
1 small lump of rock sugar or 1–2 tsp soft brown sugar
1 slice of fresh ginger
1 slice of orange

INSTRUCTIONS

Pour the sake into a small pan and set on a low heat. Gently heat for a few minutes until it's just warmed through. Pour the Mandarine Napoleon Liqueur into a heatproof cup or glass and add a small piece of rock sugar or a teaspoon of brown sugar and stir to dissolve. Pour in the warm sake and stir to mix. Taste and add more sugar if you think it needs it. Drop in the slice of fresh ginger and orange and serve.

Milk and Honey

A bedtime drink for grown-ups that I'd call nostalgic if that didn't suggest that you were sent to bed with hot brandy when you were little. The honey is actually Bénédictine, a brandy liqueur from France that's flavoured with a secret blend of herbs and spices. The liqueur is said to have soothing properties, especially for coughs and sore throats, and if the history of the drink is to be believed, was invented by Benedictine monks in the 16th century as a health elixir. Although, some people think that Alexandre Le Grand, the man who started producing Bénédictine in the 1860s, may have invented the medically minded monks to give his liqueur respectability and romance. Healing or not, the lush flavour of Bénédictine pairs perfectly with milk to make a very restorative evening drink.

250ml (8½fl oz) full-fat milk
30ml (1fl oz) Bénédictine D.O.M Liqueur
1 slice of orange
1 cinnamon stick

INSTRUCTIONS
Pour the milk into a small pan and warm over a medium heat, stirring, until it's steaming hot and just starting to bubble. Pour the Bénédictine into a heatproof glass or mug and top up with the hot milk. Stir, then garnish with a slice of orange and a cinnamon stick and serve.

Japanese Cocktail

You might be wondering why a cocktail made with Cognac, orgeat and Angostura bitters is called Japanese when there is nothing obviously Japanese about it. The name comes from the event it was created to celebrate – Japan's first diplomatic mission to the USA in 1860. Not an obvious source of inspiration for a cocktail, but the Japanese diplomats were staying in New York City, not far from a bar run by Jerry Thomas, one of America's most legendary barmen. The diplomats – especially the younger ones – took a fancy to Jerry's bar and drinks, and he repaid them the compliment by inventing this rich, aromatic drink for them.

60ml (2fl oz) Cognac
8ml (¼fl oz) orgeat syrup
2 dashes of Angostura bitters

INSTRUCTIONS
Put a coupe glass into the freezer for 30 minutes, or fill it with ice and leave it to chill for a few minutes. Put all the ingredients into a shaker, half-fill the shaker with ice, seal and give it a really good shake. Strain into the chilled glass and serve.

Cynar Spritz

This is a bridging cocktail. It carries you from summer's light and frothy Aperol Spritz to winter's cosy, syrupy glasses of Aperol *glühwein* (there's a recipe on page 97, if Hot Aperol sounds like your sort of thing). The drink gets its bittersweet flavour from the Cynar, which is an Italian liqueur flavoured with artichokes. Richer and more herbaceous than its summer cousin, the Cynar Spritz is a drink designed for colder weather aperitifs and lunches in the last of the year's sunshine.

Serves 6

300ml (10fl oz) Cynar liqueur
450ml (16fl oz) Prosecco Extra Sec, chilled
Soda water (club soda), to top up
Lemon and orange slices, to garnish

INSTRUCTIONS

Fill six large wine glasses or copa glasses with ice and add 50ml (1¾fl oz) Cynar to each glass. Pour 75ml (2½fl oz) chilled Processo into each glass and give them a quick stir. Top up with a little soda water (club soda), then drop a slice of lemon and orange into each glass and serve.

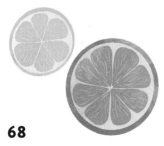

Rob Roy

You probably think that this cocktail was invented by a proud Scot, eager to celebrate the Scottish folk hero Rob Roy. But it was actually created by a barman at the Waldorf-Astoria in New York City, who'd been tasked with inventing a cocktail to publicise the first night of the operetta *Rob Roy*. The drink, first served in 1894, has long outlived that Broadway show. It's an easy-drinking twist on a Sweet Manhattan, with Scotch whisky taking the place of the bourbon. Rich and aromatic, it's a great pre-dinner drink.

60ml (2fl oz) blended Scotch whisky
30ml (1fl oz) sweet vermouth
2 dashes of Angostura bitters
Maraschino cherry, to garnish

INSTRUCTIONS
Put a coupe glass into the freezer for at least 30 minutes, or fill it with ice and leave it to chill for a few minutes. Half-fill a mixing glass with ice and pour in the whisky and vermouth. Add 2 dashes of Angostura bitters and stir well to chill, then strain into the chilled coupe glass and garnish with a maraschino cherry.

Nuts and Berries

Smart squirrels know that if autumn is good for anything, it's good for gathering nuts and berries and building up stores for chilly winter days. We can learn a lot from squirrels, especially when it comes to making sure we have a stock of essentials ready to see us through the cold months. Some people might say that hazelnut liqueurs and raspberry-scented drinks aren't really essentials, but they haven't tried this delectable dessert cocktail. It's brimming with harvest flavours and tastes a little like drinking melted ice cream. If you don't have Frangelico, it works just as well with Amaretto.

45ml (1½fl oz) Frangelico
45ml (1½fl oz) Chambord Liqueur
75ml (2½fl oz) single (light) cream

INSTRUCTIONS

Put a coupe glass into the freezer for 30 minutes, or fill it with ice and leave it to chill for a few minutes. Half-fill a mixing glass with ice and pour in the Frangelico, Chambord and the cream. Stir well to chill, then strain the cocktail into your glass and serve.

Hot Buttered Maple Bacon Bourbon

Everything is improved by adding the words 'hot buttered' to the front of it, and that's especially true of booze. The classic is Hot Buttered Rum, served strong and spicy with a silky texture thanks to the sweet butter whisked into it (turn to page 110 for a traditional recipe for Hot Buttered Rum). However, you can butter more than just rum – gin, whisky, brandy and calvados are all good choices. After a few experiments, I've settled on bacon-washed bourbon as my favourite spirit for the hot butter treatment. It was Don Lee at New York's PDT who first infused bourbon with bacon fat, and the result was a rich, smoky drink with a savoury lick of salt. Pairing it with maple-sweetened butter seems only natural, especially on long, dark winter nights.

FOR THE BACON-WASHED BOURBON:
6 rashers smoked streaky bacon with a thick layer of fat
350ml (12fl oz) bourbon

FOR THE MAPLE BUTTER:
125g (4oz) lightly salted butter, softened
75ml (2½fl oz) maple syrup
55g (2oz) dark brown soft sugar
½ tsp ground cinnamon
½ tsp allspice
¼ tsp ground cloves
A good grating of nutmeg

TO SERVE:
Boiling water

INSTRUCTIONS

To make the bacon-washed bourbon, place a heavy-based frying pan or cast-iron skillet on a low heat and gently warm it. Add the bacon rashers and slowly fry for 10–15 minutes, turning once or twice, until the fat has melted and rendered out of the bacon. Lift the crispy bacon rashers out of the pan (make a sandwich) and pour the fat into a small bowl or measuring glass. Pour the bourbon into a sterilized glass container with a wide neck (see page 18 for how to sterilize a glass jar) and add 22ml (¾fl oz) of the bacon fat. Seal and infuse at room temperature for 6 hours, then pop the jar into the freezer for 3–4 hours until the fat solidifies. Scoop the fat out of the jar. Strain the bacon-washed bourbon into a clean, sterilized bottle and store in the fridge. The bacon-washed bourbon is best used within 3–4 days.

To make the maple butter, scoop the softened butter into a bowl and add the maple syrup and brown sugar. Beat together until smoothly combined (electric beaters really help you here). Add the spices and beat again. Scoop into a tub, seal and store in the fridge. The butter will keep well for a few weeks. If you don't use it all to make drinks, then spread it on toast or use it to top pancakes.

To make the Hot Buttered Maple Bacon Bourbon, scoop 2 tablespoons maple butter into a heatproof mug or glass. Add 22ml (¾fl oz) of the bacon-washed bourbon and top up with around 100ml (3½fl oz) boiling water. Stir well to mix and serve.

Smoking Bishop

If you want to go the full Dickens this Christmas, then you need to make a hearty pan-full of Smoking Bishop, the mulled wine that Ebenezer Scrooge offers Bob Cratchit after Scrooge has learned the errors of his miserly ways. As he says in *A Christmas Carol*:

'A merrier Christmas, Bob, my good fellow, than I have given you, for many a year! I'll raise your salary, and endeavour to assist your struggling family, and we will discuss your affairs this very afternoon, over a Christmas bowl of smoking bishop, Bob!'

It is a luscious mulled wine full of festive flavours. You begin by roasting bitter Seville oranges to caramelize them. The marmalade mix of charred zest and sticky orange flesh gives the mull heart, while the 50/50 mix of red wine and fortified port wine makes sure the drink will put roses in your cheeks. Don't be tempted to boil the wine. Leave it to simmer gently, with just a little steam breaking the surface, to slowly infuse the wine with spice and sweetness.

Serves 8

3 Seville oranges (or 2 sweet oranges and
   1 lemon if you can't get hold of Sevilles)
15 whole cloves
350ml (12fl oz) ruby port
350ml (12fl oz) fruity red wine, such as Merlot or Pinot Noir
125g (4½oz) soft light brown sugar
4cm (1½in) chunk of fresh ginger
¼ tsp allspice
1 nutmeg

INSTRUCTIONS

Preheat your oven to 200°C/180°C fan/400°F/Gas mark 6.
Scrub the whole oranges to remove any wax, then stud them
with 5 cloves each. Place the oranges on a baking tray or in a
roasting tin and roast in the oven for 45 minutes until the oranges
are soft, lightly charred and caramelized. You can also roast
the oranges the day before you want to make the Smoking
Bishop and keep them in the fridge, ready to add to the pan.

When you're ready to make the Smoking Bishop, pour
the port, wine and 150ml (5¼fl oz) water into a large
pan. Tip in the sugar. Slice the ginger and add it to the
pan. Add the allspice and grate in around one-quarter
of the nutmeg. Quarter the oranges (keeping the cloves
in them) and drop the orange quarters into the pan.

Set the pan on a medium heat and warm until it's just
steaming. Pop a lid on the pan, turn the heat down to
low and gently warm for 45–60 minutes. This will help
the flavours mingle without cooking off too much of the
alcohol. Ladle the Smoking Bishop into heatproof mugs or
glasses and grate over a little more nutmeg to serve.

Vin Chaud

It's not après-ski if there isn't at least one glass of Vin Chaud on the table, ready to warm the frosty fingers of a skier who's put in a hard day on the slopes. This French version of mulled wine is less sweet than many of the other mulls dished up across Europe during the winter, and it's lightly spiced with a savoury liquorice tang. If liquorice isn't your thing, just leave out the star anise or swap it for a few slices of fresh ginger. This version is slowly simmered for around 1 hour to mingle the flavours without cooking off too much alcohol. If you like, you can make it the day before and let it sit overnight, then scoop out the oranges and spices, add in fresh orange, cinnamon and star anise, and gently warm again, ready to serve.

Serves 6

1 orange
4 whole cloves
1 cinnamon stick
1 star anise
100g (3½oz) granulated sugar
750ml (1.3 pints) red wine, such as Côtes du Rhône
75ml (2½fl oz) Cognac

INSTRUCTIONS

Quarter the orange and push a clove into each quarter. Place the orange in a large saucepan and add the cinnamon stick, star anise and sugar. Pour in the wine. Set the pan on a medium heat and warm until the wine is just steaming but not bubbling, stirring occasionally to dissolve the sugar. When the wine is steaming hot, turn the heat down to low and cover the pan with a lid. Gently heat for 1 hour. After 1 hour, pour in the Cognac and stir to mix. Ladle into mugs or heatproof glasses to serve.

Whisky Mac

The same liquid-gold colour as a sunset, and with enough warming spice to keep out any chills, the Whisky Mac is the kind of drink that makes you glad summer is over and that the time for cold-weather cocktails is here. Like any cocktail that's more than 10 years old, the Whisky Mac comes with a backstory that's one part history to two parts myth and legend. It's supposed to be named after Major-General Sir Hector Archibald MacDonald – aka Fighting Mac – a Victorian soldier who rose through the ranks to become Commander-in-Chief of the British Forces in Ceylon (now Sri Lanka). Fighting Mac was supposed to have invented the drink in India during an outbreak of cholera. Ginger was thought to have medicinal properties, so the British officers took to drinking ginger wine. Mac added whisky, to make sure the drink was extra effective, and a cocktail legend was born.

45ml (1½fl oz) blended Scotch whisky
30ml (1fl oz) Stone's Original Green Ginger Wine

INSTRUCTIONS
Pour the whisky and ginger wine into a tumbler. You can add a few ice cubes if you like, but I think it's better served at room temperature to let the flavours of the whisky breathe.

Rum and Raisin Flip

No raisins were harmed in the making of this cocktail, unless you count the dried grapes that were used to make Pedro Ximénez sherry. It's a luscious Spanish dessert wine brimming with honeyed dried fruit flavours, and it puts the festive figgy notes into this indulgent dessert cocktail. It tastes like a hard milkshake made with rum and raisin ice cream and it would make a great stand-in for dessert after a Christmas meal, or serve it by the fire at teatime when everyone is feeling celebratory but in a very gentle, slightly snoozy way.

30ml (1fl oz) dark rum
30ml (1fl oz) Pedro Ximénez sherry
60ml (2fl oz) double (heavy) cream
1 medium egg
Freshly grated nutmeg, to garnish

INSTRUCTIONS

Pour the dark rum, sherry and cream into a cocktail shaker. Crack in the egg. Shake vigorously for 30 seconds, then add a couple of ice cubes and shake again to chill. Strain into a coupe glass and grate over a little nutmeg to serve (don't skip the nutmeg – it's essential).

Penicillin

A bartender with time on their hands and a box of samples is only ever a few shakes away from creating a classic. In 2005 that bartender was Sam Ross, an Australian cocktail slinger who'd moved to New York and was working at Milk & Honey. The Compass Box had sent over a range of whiskies, and out of the pile Sam dug up a bottle of Asyla (a blended Scotch whisky) and The Peat Monster (a smoke-heavy mix of Islay and Ardmore whiskies). At the time, one of Milk & Honey's big sellers was the Gold Rush, a bourbon spin on the honey-and-lemon-laced classic the Bees Knees. Sam took the medicinal mix of lemon and honey, added a dash of sweet ginger, stirred in the whiskies, and with one pour leaped into cocktail history. If you're wondering about the name, Sam was inspired by chicken noodle soup, aka Jewish Penicillin – a dish that can cure anything, just like this drink.

22ml (¾fl oz) Honey and Ginger Syrup (see page 13)
60ml (2fl oz) blended Scotch whisky
22ml (¾fl oz) fresh lemon juice
1 tsp Islay single malt whisky
A few pieces of crystallised (candied) ginger, to garnish

INSTRUCTIONS

Make the Honey and Ginger Syrup following the recipe on page 13. Half-fill your cocktail shaker with ice and pour in the Scotch whisky, syrup and the lemon juice. Shake well to chill, then strain into an old fashioned glass filled with ice. Top with the smoky Islay whisky, then garnish with a few pieces of crystallised (candied) ginger on a cocktail pick.

Cinq à Sept

Cocktail Hour is the only hour I know that is 120 minutes long. It lasts from 5pm to 7pm and it's a golden moment in time, when the stresses and the strains of the day can be dissolved in ice-cold Martinis and Old Fashioneds while the pleasure of friends, family and dinner is anticipated. While Cocktail Hour can – and does – happen all year round, somehow it suits autumn (fall) best. Perhaps it's because those months are the bridge between summer and winter. A period of transition, just like those early evening hours spent lingering over a drink and shivering a little as night starts to fall. This cocktail is a frosty mix of gin, floral chartreuse, lemon juice and syrup that's designed to be sipped slowly with a friend or two.

60ml (2fl oz) gin
22ml (¾fl oz) lemon juice
15ml (½fl oz) Simple Syrup (see page 12)
8ml (¼fl oz) yellow chartreuse
2 dashes of tonic bitters
15ml (½fl oz) egg white
Lemon twist, to garnish

INSTRUCTIONS

Make the Simple Syrup following the recipe on page 12. Put a coupe glass into the freezer for at least 30 minutes, or fill it with ice and let it chill for a few minutes. Pour the gin, lemon juice, syrup and yellow chartreuse into a shaker. Add 2 dashes of tonic bitters and a handful of ice. Seal and shake well to chill, then strain the cocktail out into a clean glass (not the coupe) and throw away the ice. Pour the cocktail back into the shaker and add the egg white. Seal and shake really well to foam the egg white (it forms a better foam if you shake it without the ice). Strain the cocktail into the chilled coupe and garnish with a lemon twist.

Caribou

In Quebec they say that this warming winter drink got its name when French trappers took to mixing hot, fresh caribou blood with red wine to fortify them on long hunts in the frozen Canadian wilderness. It's a good, gory story and it entertains the tourists, who sip shots of Caribou, then feel inspired to dance in the winter parades. But it's not true, of course. Or, at least, I don't think it's true. One thing I am sure of is that nothing will keep you warm like a glass of Caribou. It's strong stuff, designed to stop drinkers feeling the cold while enjoying Quebec's winter carnival, so it's best served in small measures.

Serves 8
750ml (1.3 pints) medium-bodied red wine, such as Merlot
250ml (8½fl oz) Canadian rye whisky
120ml (4fl oz) maple syrup

INSTRUCTIONS
Pour the red wine and rye whisky into a large pan, then pour in the maple syrup. Set the pan on a medium heat, pop on a lid and warm until the pan is just steaming hot. Turn the heat down and gently warm for 10–15 minutes. Ladle the Caribou into small heatproof glasses or cups and serve. Alternatively, let the Caribou cool, then chill and serve over ice.

Hot Gin Punch

In the 18th century, stalls in London used to sell hot gin and gingerbread during the frost fairs held on the frozen River Thames. It's been 200 years since the Thames was iced up enough to support a few thousand revellers, but with a glass of this Hot Gin Punch we can recreate the experience inside our cosy modern homes without even turning down the thermostat. As a drink, it's heavy on the citrus and cloves, so it does taste like it's doing you some good. It is very strong, though, so serve it in small glasses. I used Old Tom gin to recreate that malty flavour familiar to 18th-century gin drinkers, but this works just as well with your favourite London dry or artisanal gin. If you're wondering what to serve with this punch, it really goes well with ginger biscuits.

Serves 8–10

120ml (4fl oz) Lemon and Honey Syrup
    (see page 13), plus extra to serve
1 orange
1 lemon
10 whole cloves
350ml (12fl oz) Old Tom gin
350ml (12fl oz) Marsala wine
Freshly grated nutmeg, to serve

INSTRUCTIONS

Make the Lemon and Honey Syrup following the recipe on page 13. Slice the orange and lemon and stud a few slices with the cloves. Pop in a large pan and pour in 120ml (4fl oz) of the prepared syrup. Add the gin and Marsala wine. Set the pan on a medium heat and warm until steaming hot. Turn the heat down to low, pop a lid on the pan and gently warm for 20–25 minutes to mingle the flavours. Ladle the Hot Gin Punch into small heatproof glasses, grate over a little nutmeg and serve. Keep a jug of extra Lemon and Honey Syrup ready, to add extra to drinks.

Brandy Alexander

Alexander cocktails were originally made with gin, but in the 1930s, some bright spark ditched the juniper in favour of a shot glass full of brandy and barflies across America fell instantly in love. The gin version was confined to the dumpster of history and it's the Brandy Alexander that has dominated menus around the world ever since. The perfect dessert cocktail, the Brandy Alexander is a rich and creamy concoction with a subtle chocolate flavour that's elevated by the dusting of nutmeg and cinnamon added just before serving. They enhance the cocktail's richness and bring a note of delicious winter spice. The other key ingredient in a good Brandy Alexander is elbow grease. This is a drink that benefits from a really good shake. In his 1937 cocktail compendium *Famous New Orleans Drinks and How To Mix 'Em*, Stanley Arthur adds this note to his Brandy Alexander recipe: 'Be strenuous in your shaking whenever there is white of egg or cream in a mixture. Shake, brother, shake, and then shake some more for good measure.' Shake for long enough and, in Arthur's words, you'll have a drink that's as 'smooth as cream, as delicate as dew'.

45ml (1½fl oz) Cognac
30ml (1fl oz) dark crème de cacao
30ml (1fl oz) single (light) cream
15ml (½fl oz) egg white
Freshly grated nutmeg and ground cinnamon, to garnish

INSTRUCTIONS
Put a coupe glass into the freezer for 30 minutes, or fill it with ice and leave it to chill for a few minutes. Pour the Cognac, dark crème de cacao, cream and egg white into a shaker, then add a handful of ice and give it a really good shake. Strain into the chilled glass and serve dusted with a little freshly grated nutmeg and a small pinch of cinnamon.

94

Hot Aperol Spritz

If you're walking around a Christmas market in Germany or Northern Italy and you catch a waft of something a little more tropical than the typical cinnamon-spiced *glühwein*, there's probably a stall somewhere selling Hot Aperol Spritz. A winter version of the summer Spritz, this mulled wine is full of juicy fruit flavours thanks to the mix of mango syrup (which you should be able to find in speciality liquor stores or coffee suppliers), apple juice and fresh orange. It's perfect for sipping on a winter stroll or serving at a party if you want something lighter and fresher than the usual mulled wines.

Serves 8

1 orange
200ml (7fl oz) Aperol
750ml (1.3 pints) white wine, such as a dry Riesling
300ml (10fl oz) apple juice
75ml (2½fl oz) mango syrup

INSTRUCTIONS

Slice the orange and tip it into a large pan. Pour in the Aperol, white wine, apple juice and mango syrup. Set the pan on a medium heat and warm until the pan is steaming hot. Turn the heat down to low, pop a lid on the pan and gently warm for 10–15 minutes to mingle the flavours. Ladle the Hot Aperol Spritz into heatproof mugs or glasses and serve.

Tom and Jerry

One of Eggnog's many descendants, the Tom and Jerry is a frothy concoction of eggs, butter, spices, rum and Cognac, which you top up with either hot water or warm milk, depending on how rich and creamy you'd like your drink to be. The batter takes about 10 minutes to make but it keeps well in the fridge, making it an ideal prepare-ahead party drink. As far as the name goes, there is a connection to a mouse (but no cartoon cat, alas). The 19th-century cocktail legend 'Professor' Jerry Thomas laid claim to the recipe in the 1840s, spinning a yarn about how he invented it for a man who came to his bar in need of sustenance and then named the drink after his pet mice – Tom and Jerry – who were, of course, named after Jerry Thomas himself. But descriptions of spiced rum and egg drinks have been traced back to the 1820s, before Jerry Thomas was even born, so the Professor may have been overstating his inventiveness. Given how delicious the drink is, I can't blame him for trying to claim it.

Serves 6

FOR THE BATTER:

2 medium eggs
100g (3½oz) caster (superfine) sugar
60g (2oz) unsalted butter, softened
1 tbsp dark rum
½ tsp ground cinnamon
½ tsp ground cloves
½ tsp freshly grated nutmeg

FOR THE DRINK:

180ml (6fl oz) dark rum
180ml (6fl oz) brandy
Boiling water or warm milk, to top up
Freshly grated nutmeg, to serve

Make the batter by separating the eggs – put the whites in a clean glass or metal bowl, and the yolks into a large mixing bowl. Add the sugar, softened butter and rum to the egg yolks and beat until smooth and combined. Add the cinnamon, cloves and nutmeg to the bowl and beat to mix them in. Set aside.

Whisk the eggs whites until soft peaks form, then use a tablespoon or spatula to fold the egg whites into the buttery egg yolks. You can use the batter straight away, or transfer the batter to a container, seal and store in the fridge for up to 1 week.

When you're ready to make the drinks, spoon 2 tablespoons of the batter into 6 heatproof glasses or mugs. Add 30ml (1fl oz) dark rum and Cognac to each glass. Top up with around 100ml (3½fl oz) boiling water or warm milk each, stirring as you add it so you get a smoothly combined drink with a slightly foamy top. Grate over a little nutmeg and serve.

Through the Wardrobe

This cocktail was inspired by one of my favourite winter-set books, *The Lion, The Witch and The Wardrobe*. In the first chapter, Lucy walks into a wardrobe in a rambling English country house and steps out into a frost-dipped forest in Narnia, the land where it's always winter and never Christmas. I wanted to capture that moment, when Lucy first breathes in the cold night air of Narnia, sparkling with ice and magic. The herby bitterness of the Suze combined with the pine syrup and juniper-heavy gin are the trees while the egg white is the fluffy falling snow. Suze is a syrupy French aperitif flavoured with gentian root, which gives it a honeyed bitterness with a hint of orange. If you can't find it, you can swap in Cocchi Americano Bianco or Fernet-Branca. While you can make a pine syrup by simmering cuttings from an edible pine in Simple Syrup (see page 12 for recipe), it is easier and safer to buy pine syrup from speciality wine and spirit shops or coffee shops.

1 tsp Suze
60ml (2fl oz) gin
22ml (¾fl oz) pine syrup

22ml (¾fl oz) lime juice
15ml (½fl oz) egg white
Lime twist, to garnish

INSTRUCTIONS

Chill a coupe glass in the freezer for 30 minutes, or fill it with ice and leave it to chill for a few minutes. To make the cocktail, pour the Suze into the cold glass, tip it 45 degrees and turn it to lightly coat it with the liqueur. Tip out any excess. Pour the gin, pine syrup and lime juice into a cocktail shaker with a handful of ice. Seal and shake well, then strain into a clean, empty glass (not your coupe). Discard the ice and pour the cocktail back into the shaker. Add the egg white and shake well for 30 seconds or so (shaking the egg white without the ice helps to make it fluffy). Drop a lime twist into the chilled coupe glass, then strain in the cocktail and serve.

Hot Peppermint Patty

'Oh my god, you have to try this! Hot cocoa, dark crème de cacao, hint of crème de menthe and peppermint schnapps. I call it a Peppermint Patty.' So says Sterling Archer, the world's greatest spy and a man who never lets a mission stop him from taking time out to enjoy a steaming hot mug of the good stuff. The star of his own FX cartoon sitcom, Archer is an inspiration to drinkers and a challenge to bar staff the world over. After the Peppermint Patty episode of the show aired, fans of the series devoted themselves to working out the exact proportions of Archer's spiked hot chocolate. This version is rich, decadent and just the right side of dangerous, a little like Archer himself.

3 heaped tsp cocoa powder
250ml (8½fl oz) full-fat milk
22ml (¾fl oz) white peppermint schnapps
22ml (¾fl oz) dark crème de cacao
8ml (¼fl oz) crème de menthe
Whipped (heavy) cream (or squirty cream)
    and grated chocolate, to garnish

INSTRUCTIONS
Measure out the cocoa powder in a heatproof bowl or saucepan, whisk in the milk and heat it up – in the microwave or on the hob, whichever works best for you. In a separate heatproof mug, measure out the peppermint schnapps, dark crème de cacao and crème de menthe. When the hot chocolate is ready, pour it over the peppermint schnapps mix and stir to combine. Spoon (or squirt) some whipped cream on top of the hot chocolate and grate over a little chocolate to serve.

Il Bombardino

Once upon a time on a mountain in Italy, four skiers were caught in a blizzard. Lucky for them they were caught in a blizzard not far from a cosy ski lodge. Even luckier, the owner was a dab hand at mixing drinks. So when they stumbled into the lodge, wet and bedraggled, the barman set to work, heating up a pan of zabaglione and whisky, pouring it into espresso cups and topping it generously with whipped cream. The shivering skiers gathered round and when the first skier took a sip, he slapped the table and cried: '*Accidenti! È una bomba!*' ('Damn! It's a bomb!') And that is how the Bombardino got its name. Over the years it's evolved into a mix of egg liqueur, brandy and cream, and there is a variation that includes a shot of espresso – called a Calimero – for skiers who want a drink that will wake, as well as warm, them up.

Serves 4

200ml (7fl oz) Advocaat
45ml (1½fl oz) brandy
80ml (2¾fl oz) fresh espresso (optional)
Whipped (heavy) cream (or squirty cream)
    and cocoa powder, to serve

INSTRUCTIONS

Pour the Advocaat and brandy into a small pan and warm over a gentle heat, stirring, for a couple of minutes until steaming hot. Pour the hot Advocaat into four espresso cups. If you're adding coffee, pour a fresh shot of espresso into each cup – it should float on top of the Advocaat. Top with a swirl of whipped cream and dust over a little cocoa powder to serve.

Hot Toddy

Famously there is no known cure for the common cold, but a Hot Toddy does seem to help. Why this drink seems to work when everything else fails is a mystery. It could be down to the slice of lemon, which is full of vitamin C and said to ease the symptoms of a cold. It might be the honey, a natural antibiotic that soothes sore throats and coughs. Perhaps it's because of the cloves, which taste medicinal and therefore must be doing you some good. Or maybe it's the whisky, which is no use at all from a medical perspective but, goodness, it does make you feel better.

1 slice of lemon
2 whole cloves
35ml (1¼fl oz) blended Scotch whisky
1 tbsp lemon juice
1 tbsp honey
Boiling water, to top up

INSTRUCTIONS
Stud the slice of lemon with the whole cloves. Pour the whisky into a mug or heatproof glass and add the lemon juice and honey. Drop in the lemon slice. Top up the mug with around 100–150ml (3½–5¼fl oz) boiling water and stir to dissolve the honey. Serve immediately.

Mulled Sloe Gin

Sticky and sweet, sloe gin is a winter favourite. I've often drunk sloe gin, cold and syrupy, over ice or mixed it with soda and lime for a longer drink, but it had never occurred to me to try drinking it warm. Then gin distillers Sipsmith took a new cocktail to London's Christmas markets: Mulled Sloe Gin. They warmed sloe gin with apple juice and fistfuls of spices, and a classic Christmas drink was born. This is my version, which has a little lemon juice to balance out the sweetness and cloves and cinnamon for spice. You can experiment with your favourite spices: star anise, cardamom, vanilla and ginger are all worth adding to the pot.

22ml (¾fl oz) sloe gin (shop-bought or homemade, see page 16)
250ml (8½fl oz) apple juice
1 tbsp lemon juice
1 slice of orange
2 whole cloves
1 cinnamon stick

INSTRUCTIONS
Pour the sloe gin, apple juice and lemon juice into a small pan. Stud the orange slice with the cloves and drop it into the pan with the cinnamon stick. Place on a medium heat, pop on a lid and gently warm, stirring occasionally, until steaming hot. Pour into a heatproof glass or mug and serve.

Hot Buttered Rum

A hug of a drink that will warm you from the inside out, Hot Buttered Rum has been doling out winter cheer for hundreds of years. The mix of butter, sugar and spices tastes like spreadable gingerbread and, stirred with golden rum and hot water, creates a silky and indulgent drink. No golden rum? Try it with dark or white rum – or with gin, brandy, whisky or any spirit you think would benefit from a liberal buttering and plenty of spice.

1 tbsp lightly salted butter, softened
2 tsp soft light brown sugar
A pinch of ground cinnamon
A pinch of ground nutmeg
A pinch of allspice
A pinch of ground cloves
35ml (1¼fl oz) golden rum
Boiling water, to top up
Cinnamon stick, to serve

INSTRUCTIONS

Scoop the butter into a small bowl and add the sugar and the spices. Mash together until smoothly combined, then scoop the spiced butter into a heatproof glass or mug. Pour in the golden rum and top up with about 100ml (3½fl oz) boiling water. Stir well until it's smoothly combined, then taste and add a pinch more of the spices or sugar if you think it needs it. Drop in a cinnamon stick and serve.

Black Velvet

A tray of Black Velvet cocktails is often brought out for St Patrick's Day parties, but it's actually a drink with a dark origin story that dates back to the 14 December 1861 – the day Prince Albert died. The husband of Queen Victoria, he died young and left her a widow aged just 42. The day he died she changed into her widow's clothing and stayed in mourning for the rest of her life. Albert's death cast a gloom over Britain and a barman at Brooks Club in London decided that even the drinks should be shrouded in black, so he created the Black Velvet – a sombre Champagne cocktail to commemorate the Prince. It's a moody sip that pairs well with oysters, candlelit parties and spooky tales.

Serves 6
720ml (1.25 pints) Brut Champagne, chilled
300ml (10fl oz) Guinness Original Stout Beer

INSTRUCTIONS
Pour 125ml (4fl oz) of chilled Champagne into each of six flute glasses and then pour 50ml (1¾fl oz) chilled Guinness into each glass. Guinness is heavier than Champagne, so it will sink through the Champagne and they'll mix together. If you'd like to serve layered Black Velvets, start by pouring the Champagne into the glasses, then slowly pour the Guinness over the back of a bar spoon or teaspoon to float it on top of the Champagne.

Ponche de Crème

A creamy drink spiked with a generous quantity of rum is a Caribbean Christmas must-have. Ponche de Crème – also known as Ponche-a-Crème and Poncha Crema – is Trinidad's contribution to the festive drinks' cabinet. The addition of lime and Angostura bitters adds a zestiness that makes it fresher and lighter than the rich and creamy Eggnogs you find in North America. It will keep in the fridge for 2–3 days and the flavour mellows, so it's worth making the day before to give it time to relax. If you're worried about serving a drink made with raw egg yolks, look out for cartons of pasteurized yolks in larger supermarkets. Use around 170g (6oz) pasteurized egg yolk as the base for the cocktail, and just follow the recipe.

Serves 6–8

4 medium egg yolks
Finely grated zest of 1 lime
397g (14oz) tin of condensed milk
400ml (14fl oz) tin of evaporated milk
300ml (10fl oz) white rum
2 tsp Angostura bitters
½ nutmeg, plus extra to serve

INSTRUCTIONS

Separate the egg yolks from the whites. The whites can be set aside for meringues (they freeze really well). Tip the yolks into a large bowl and add the lime zest. Whisk together for a few minutes until the eggs are light and fluffy (an electric whisk will save you a lot of labour). Slowly pour in the condensed milk, whisking well, then do the same with the evaporated milk. Slowly whisk in the rum. Pour in the Angostura bitters and grate in the nutmeg. Whisk again until smooth, then taste and add a little more Angostura or nutmeg if needed. Pour through a fine-mesh sieve into a jug. To serve, fill tumblers with ice, pour in the Ponche de Crème and dust with a little extra nutmeg.

Chocolate Orange-tini

I don't think I could have got more chocolate into this cocktail, short of just blitzing all the ingredients in a blender with a bar of the good stuff. There are two types of crème de cacao in this dessert drink – rich and heavy dark crème de cacao and the lighter, brighter white crème de cacao. Plus a dash or two of chocolate bitters and a pinch of grated chocolate to decorate the glass. But cocktail lovers cannot live by chocolate alone, so the citrusy bite of the triple sec offsets the richness of all the chocolate (and cream), giving the drink a subtle hint of orange.

2 tbsp Simple Syrup (see page 12)
5g (¼oz) 70% cocoa dark chocolate
45ml (1½fl oz) single (light) cream
22ml (¾fl oz) dark crème de cacao
22ml (¾fl oz) white crème de cacao
30ml (1fl oz) triple sec
2 dashes of chocolate bitters
Orange twist, to garnish

INSTRUCTIONS
Make the Simple Syrup following the recipe on page 12. Coarsely grate the chocolate onto a plate. Pour 1 tablespoon of the simple syrup onto a separate plate. Dip the rim of a martini or coupe glass into the syrup and then into the grated chocolate to coat it. Pop the glass in the fridge to chill while you make the cocktail. Pour the remaining syrup into a cocktail shaker and add the cream, both types of crème de cacao, the triple sec and 2 dashes of chocolate bitters. Add a handful of ice. Seal and shake well to chill. Strain the cocktail into the chilled glass and garnish with an orange twist to serve.

Mulled Wine Martini

There's more than one way to mull a wine. This ice-cold Martini is made with a dash of Simple Syrup mulled with festive spices and stirred with vodka, a fruity ruby port and a citrusy spoonful of triple sec. It tastes exactly like mulled wine but without all the steam and heat, although it is still pretty warming. For a party you could scale up the recipe and stir the Martini with ice, then strain into jugs, ready to pour.

10ml (¼fl oz) Mulled Wine Spice Syrup (see page 15)
50ml (1¾fl oz) vodka
30ml (1fl oz) ruby port
15ml (½fl oz) triple sec
2 dashes of orange bitters
Orange twist, to garnish

INSTRUCTIONS

Make the Mulled Wine Spice Syrup following the recipe on page 15. Put a martini glass into the freezer for at least 30 minutes, or fill it with ice and leave to chill for a few minutes. Pour the spice syrup, vodka, port and triple sec into a mixing glass half-filled with ice, then add 2 dashes of orange bitters. Stir well for at least 30 seconds to chill. Strain into the chilled glass and serve, garnished with an orange twist.

Sugar Cookie Cocktail

Yes, you can bake sugar cookies for Christmas. You can bake them so you're ready with snacks for the carol singers that come to your door, or fill a box with them to take to the school play to dazzle the other parents with. You can bake a tray of sugar cookies to hang on the Christmas tree or to nibble on while you get stuck into the gift-wrapping. You can definitely bake lots of sugar cookies this Christmas. And they are very nice. But aren't they a little bit nicer when they're drinkable? By drinkable I mean recreated as a cocktail. This dessert drink tastes exactly like a vanilla-scented sugar cookie and comes with a pleasingly over-the-top sugar-sprinkle-decorated glass. It is slightly ridiculous, definitely extravagant and wonderfully indulgent, which all the best festive treats are.

1 tbsp Simple Syrup (see page 12)
2 tsp sugar sprinkles
22ml (¾fl oz) vanilla vodka
22ml (¾fl oz) Frangelico
50ml (1¾fl oz) Baileys Irish Cream
15ml (½fl oz) double (heavy) cream

INSTRUCTIONS

Make the Simple Syrup following the recipe on page 12. Pour 1 tablespoon of the syrup onto a plate and sprinkle the sugar sprinkles onto a separate plate. Dip the rim of a martini or coupe glass into the syrup and then into the sprinkles to coat it. Pop the glass in the fridge to chill while you make the cocktail. Pour the vanilla vodka, Frangelico, Baileys and cream into a cocktail shaker and add a handful of ice. Seal and shake well to chill. Strain the cocktail into the chilled glass and serve.

Home Fires

In December 2019 I got on a train to go home for Christmas. I was carrying a suitcase full of gifts, a miniature Christmas tree nicknamed Sidney and my laptop, because I wanted to start working on my new book *Winter Warmers*. The train left London and I was quickly absorbed in my work. A little too absorbed, because I didn't notice the train split in half or that I was in the half heading in the wrong direction. Eventually, when I did realize, I panicked and scrambled off the train, finding myself in a small, dark, empty station with no idea how to get home. Thank goodness for mobile phones and my sister Alex, who knows that train network backwards. She navigated me home until I was back where I was supposed to be, with a drink in my hand and a fire warming my toes. This cocktail, made with some of Alex's favourite spirits, commemorates that night. It tastes like a buttery almond tart eaten by the fireside and is best enjoyed with the people you love.

1 tsp Islay single malt whisky
60ml (2fl oz) bourbon
22ml (¾fl oz) Amaretto
15ml (½fl oz) Pedro Ximenez sherry
22ml (¾fl oz) lemon juice
2 dashes of aromatic bitters
Maraschino cherry, to garnish

INSTRUCTIONS

Put a coupe glass into the freezer for at least 30 minutes, or fill it with ice and let it chill for a few minutes. Pour the whisky into the chilled glass, tilt it and turn it round a few times to coat with the whisky. Set to one side. Pour the bourbon, Amaretto, sherry and lemon juice into a shaker and add a handful of ice. Add 2 dashes of aromatic bitters and shake well to chill. Strain into the glass with the whisky and serve, garnished with a maraschino cherry.

Bellerina

I was introduced to potato latkes with sour cream and apple sauce by my friend Jo Bell, who has taken me to several Chanukah parties over the years. Parties where I never fail to do justice to the latkes – as well as the doughnuts and cheesecake – and usually lose at playing dreidel. When I was trying to imagine the perfect drink to go with latkes, I began to wonder about beetroot. Its earthy sweetness would pair perfectly with the crisp fried potatoes, the apple sauce and the cream. Add in a little heat from horseradish vodka (or a simple, good-quality vodka if you can't find horseradish-flavoured vodka in your local liquor store) and warmth from ginger beer and the cocktail was almost made. The final drink is light, crisp and a delicate pink. The perfect plate mate for my favourite festive fried foods.

15ml (½fl oz) Beetroot Syrup (see page 14)
45ml (1½fl oz) horseradish vodka
15ml (½fl oz) fresh lime juice
75ml (2½fl oz) apple juice
75ml (2½fl oz) ginger beer
Lime wedge, to garnish

INSTRUCTIONS
Make the Beetroot Syrup following the recipe on page 14. Pour the syrup, horseradish vodka and lime juice into a shaker, then add a couple of ice cubes and give it a really good shake. Fill a highball glass with ice and strain the cocktail into it. Add the apple juice and ginger beer, then give the mix a stir. Drop in a lime wedge and serve.

Snowball

Pity the poor Snowball. Once the height of fashion, these days it's locked out of the party. It's a very unfair fate for a fun and refreshing drink. Perhaps if it hadn't been fashionable in the 1970s, the decade that good taste notoriously forgot, people would be more willing to give it a shot. But it's stuck with its tacky '70s reputation – unless we rescue it? I think we should try. As a long drink, it's light, fizzy and has a creamy edge, a little like a grown-up cream soda. It's brilliant for parties because it's quick and easy to make and I think a tray loaded with Snowballs is a great way to greet your guests, whatever you're celebrating.

15ml (½fl oz) fresh lime juice
45ml (1½fl oz) Advocaat
100ml (3½fl oz) good-quality lemonade
Maraschino cherry, to garnish

INSTRUCTIONS
Fill a highball glass with ice. Pour in the lime juice and Advocaat, then pour in the lemonade, gently stirring as you add it so the drink develops a light froth on top (the snow in your Snowball). Drop a maraschino cherry into the glass and serve.

Frostbite

When Jack Frost is nipping at your toes, warm up with a Frostbite. It's surprisingly refreshing for a drink made with a mix of silver tequila, crème de cacao, blue curaçao and double (heavy) cream. Somehow the savouriness of the tequila stops the sweetness from getting out of hand, which makes this a great dessert cocktail for people who don't really like sweet stuff. If drinking a blue cocktail is a bit too kitsch for you, swap it for normal triple sec (although blue cocktails are more fun).

45ml (1½fl oz) silver tequila
22ml (¾fl oz) blue curaçao
22ml (¾fl oz) crème de cacao white
30ml (1fl oz) double (heavy) cream
Maraschino cherry, to garnish

INSTRUCTIONS
Fill a cocktail shaker with ice and pour in all the ingredients. Shake well to chill. Add a few ice cubes to a tumbler, then strain the cocktail into the glass. Drop in a maraschino cherry to garnish and serve.

Gin Daisy

Tom Bullock was the first African-American bartender to write a cocktail book. Published in 1917, *The Ideal Bartender* is a treasure-trove of pre-Prohibition American cocktails and the distillation of Bullock's 25 years behind the bar at the St Louis Country Club, Missouri. Bullock's reputation as a bartender there was so great that when a certain Colonel Theodore Roosevelt tried to prove how sober he was by claiming to have only drunk a few sips of a Mint Julep in the club, the *St Louis Post-Dispatch* scoffed: 'Who was ever known to drink just a part of one of Tom's?... To believe that a red-blooded man, and a true Colonel at that, ever stopped with just a part of one of those refreshments... is to strain credulity too far.' *The Ideal Bartender* includes a recipe for a Kentucky-style Mint Julep, made simply with sugar, water, bourbon and 'a bouquet of mint', but the range of gin cocktails is what draws me in. Bullock was especially fond of Old Tom gin, the sweet and malty style of gin that predated the now more familiar London dry, and his Gin Daisy is a refreshing and light drink with a dash of sherbet to it. It is easy to make in larger quantities, so if you're looking for a drink to serve at Kwanzaa festivities, why not make it one of Tom's?

15ml (½fl oz) fresh lime juice
30ml (1fl oz) grenadine
45ml (1½fl oz) Old Tom gin
Soda water (club soda), to top up
Lime wedge and mint sprigs, to garnish

INSTRUCTIONS
Fill a Collins glass or tankard with ice. Pour in the lime juice, grenadine and Old Tom gin and give them a gentle stir to mix. Top up with soda water, stir and garnish with a wedge of lime and a few mint sprigs.

Eggnog

A boozy milkshake straight in from the 18th century, Eggnog is as much a part of the holiday season as Christmas trees, candy canes and thinking karaoke is a good idea at the office Christmas party. As a drink, it can trace its history back to medieval monks warming their bones with hot possets of eggs, ale and cream. Over the centuries Eggnogs have gone through a few evolutions until we get to the creamily indulgent drink that we love today. Serve over ice with a good dusting of nutmeg, and if you don't have any Cognac, use dark rum instead.

15ml (½fl oz) Simple Syrup (see page 12)
50ml (1¾fl oz) Cognac
50ml (1¾fl oz) double (heavy) cream
65ml (2¼fl oz) full-fat milk
1 small egg
Freshly grated nutmeg, to garnish

INSTRUCTIONS

Make the Simple Syrup following the recipe on page 12. Pour the Cognac, prepared syrup, cream and milk into a cocktail shaker. Crack in the egg. Shake vigorously for around 30 seconds, then add a couple of ice cubes and shake again to chill. Add a few ice cubes to a tumbler, then strain the Eggnog into the glass. Grate over a little fresh nutmeg to serve.

Candy Cane Martini

When faced with a pile of presents to wrap, I like to reach for a drink. Gift-wrapping is much more fun with a Martini by your side, and the right amount of Martini can often result in inspired ribbon arrangements and creative gift-tag messages. This particular Martini is ridiculously festive and generously portioned – don't expect to get through more than two. When you're picking a bottle of crème de menthe, choose a clear crème de menthe if you can. The classic green version will taste just as nice, but it will give your cocktail a distinctly Grinch-like hue.

45ml (1½fl oz) vodka
45ml (1½fl oz) white crème de cacao
22ml (¾fl oz) crème de menthe
Crushed candy cane, to serve (optional)

INSTRUCTIONS

If you like a bit extra when it comes to garnishing cocktails, don't save your candy cane to serve on the side of your Martini. Instead, use this optional decoration suggestion. Break a small chunk off and bash it with a rolling pin or blitz it into a food processor to crush it, then sprinkle it on a plate. Dip the rim of a martini glass in some Simple Syrup (see page 12), then put the glass in the fridge while you make the drink.

If you're not feeling that extravagant and would rather stick to a more traditional drink, simply put a martini glass into the freezer for 30 minutes, or fill it with ice and leave it to chill for a few minutes.

Pour all the ingredients into a mixing glass, half-fill with ice and stir for around 30 seconds to chill. Strain into the chilled glass and serve, garnished with a small candy cane.

After Midnight

There are two key things to remember when mixing a cocktail for New Year's Eve: it must be fizzy and it must be easy to make. No one wants to get stuck behind the bar when the clocks begin to strike midnight. Not when there's dancing, kissing and *Auld Lang Syne* to sing. This wintry take on a Kir Royale is the perfect fit for New Year parties. Rich and indulgent, it takes seconds to make. For an extra kick you can add a tablespoon of brandy, but only if you think your party needs a bit of extra swing.

1 tbsp crème de figue
2 dashes of Angostura bitters
Chilled Brut Champagne, to top up

INSTRUCTIONS
Pour the crème de figue into a flute glass. Add the Angostura bitters, then top up with chilled Champagne to serve.

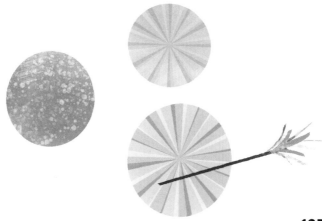

Endless Night

In the depths of winter it can sometimes feel like the nights are never going to end, which is why – here in the Northern Hemisphere – I always find 21 December cheering. It may be the longest night of the year, but every day after that is one day closer to the long hot days of summer. So I like to celebrate the Winter Equinox with a suitably long, dark drink. This raven-hued cocktail is based on a Black Russian but with dark rum swapped in for vodka to make sure that every element of the drink is dark and gloomy, and also to give it an extra layer of molasses-rich sweetness.

22ml (¾fl oz) dark rum
22ml (¾fl oz) Kahlua
2–3 dashes of Angostura bitters
Chilled Coca-Cola, to top up

INSTRUCTIONS
Fill a highball glass with ice. Pour in the dark rum and Kahlua. Shake in 2–3 dashes of Angostura bitters. Top up with Coca-Cola and serve.

Café Amore

Every café in Paris has at least one liqueur coffee on its menu. Normally a whisky-laden Irish coffee that's served with a thick layer of cream floating on the top. But if you're lucky, as I once was, you'll get caught in the rain and stumble into a gilded Belle Epoque café, cold and wet, only to discover that the *cartes des boissons* has a whole section devoted to warming, boozy coffees. There were Caribbean coffees with rum, Norman coffees with calvados, American coffees with bourbon, Italian coffees with grappa, and a Café Amore, a coffee for lovers made with sweet amaretto and a shot of Cognac. Intense, aromatic and indulgent, it's the coffee your Valentine's Day date has been waiting for.

Serves 2

50ml (1¾fl oz) Cognac
50ml (1¾fl oz) amaretto
400ml (14fl oz) hot filter coffee
Whipped (heavy) cream (or squirty cream)
    and flaked almonds, to serve

Instructions

Pour the Cognac and amaretto into 2 heatproof mugs or glasses. Pour in the hot coffee and stir to mix. Top with plenty of whipped cream and a sprinkle of flaked almonds.

Index

143

Acknowledgements

Thank you to all my drinking partners who shared their favourite drinks with me – and also put in a few requests. In particular, to Naomi and Andrew Knill, Nicola Swift, Francesca Burnett-Hall, Jennie Brotherston and Jordi Morrison, Jo Bell; my sisters Alex and Cara Davis; and my parents Gerry and Doug, who were there with the back-up Baileys supplies just when mine ran out.

Thank you to Sarah Ferone for the stunning illustrations that brought the cocktails to festive light, and to Jacqui Caulton, as ever, for her brilliant design. Thanks to Charlotte Cross and Mike Jones for their continued enthusiasm for this project, and to Abi Waters, Helena Caldon and Ben Murphy for perfecting this project on the page.